CORAL REEFS

A WHOLE NEW WORLD UNDER THE SEA

Nature Encyclopedia for Kids
Children's Nature Books

BABY PROFESSOR
EDUCATION KIDS

Speedy Publishing LLC
40 E. Main St. #1156
Newark, DE 19711
www.speedypublishing.com

Copyright © 2017

Have you ever seen a coral reef in an aquarium or in the ocean? Did you realize that it was a living organism? It is considered to be one of the major marine biomes. While it is a fairly small biome, approximately 25% of the marine species make these reefs their homes. The coral reef is considered an aquatic biome. In this book, you will be learning about the marine biome known as the coral reef. First, we will provide a brief overview of the Ecosystem, Biome, and Marine Biome so that you will have a greater understanding as to how these beautiful reefs are created.

Great Barrier Reef.

ECOSYSTEM

A certain area where a living organism interacts with each other, as well as with the air, the sun, and the water is called an ecosystem. These living organisms working together in a specific area are known as a unit. It can be miles of a desert, or a bubble of water. Each one is unique and has established its balance over time which is of importance to each life form.

BIOME

This describes a larger group of comparable ecosystems. They each will be consisting of similar plants, animals, rainfall, and weather. There are many biomes on Earth. Some examples of biomes are Grasslands, Desert, Tundra, Savanna, Tundra, Tropical Rainforest, Temperate Forest, and Taiga Forest. Examples of aquatic biomes include Marine, Freshwater, and Coral Reefs.

Aerial view coral outcrop great barrier reef Queensland.

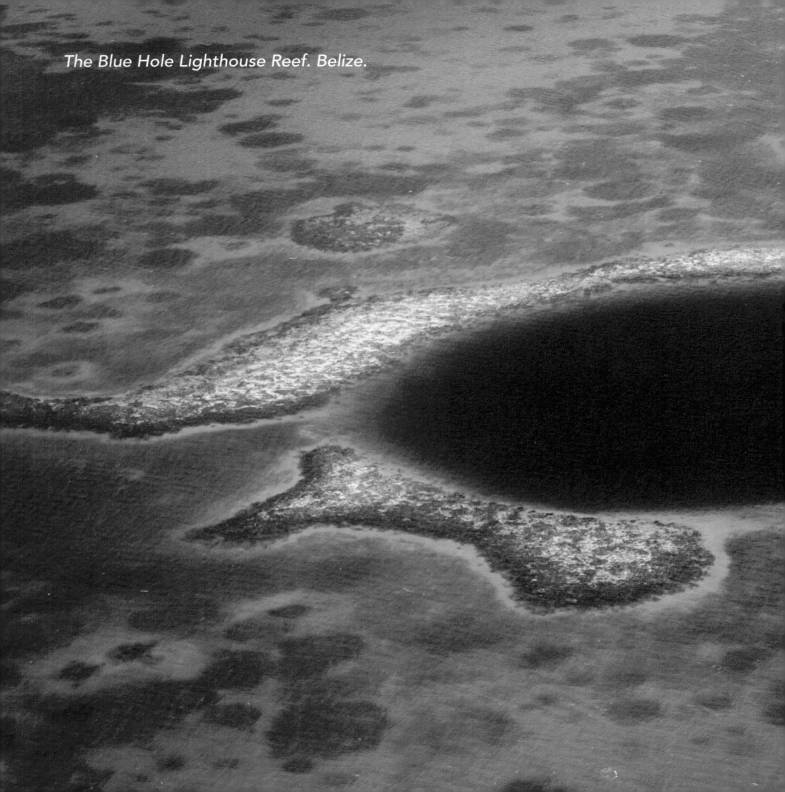

The Blue Hole Lighthouse Reef. Belize.

MARINE BIOMES

The two major aquatic biomes are the marine and freshwater biomes. The marine biome consists primarily of saltwater oceans. This is the largest biome on Earth and this planet is covered by about 70% of saltwater oceans.

Even though a marine biome is made primarily of our oceans, there are three different types:

OCEANS – There are basically five oceans that cover the planet, including the Southern, Artic, Indian, Pacific, and Atlantic.

CORAL REEFS – These reefs are smaller than oceans, but approximately 25% of marine species live in these reefs making them a vital biome.

ESTUARIES - These are areas where streams and rivers flow into our oceans. This then creates an ecosystem or biome with fascinating and distinct animal and plant life.

Aerial view of the underwater waterfall and Le Morne Brabant peninsula.

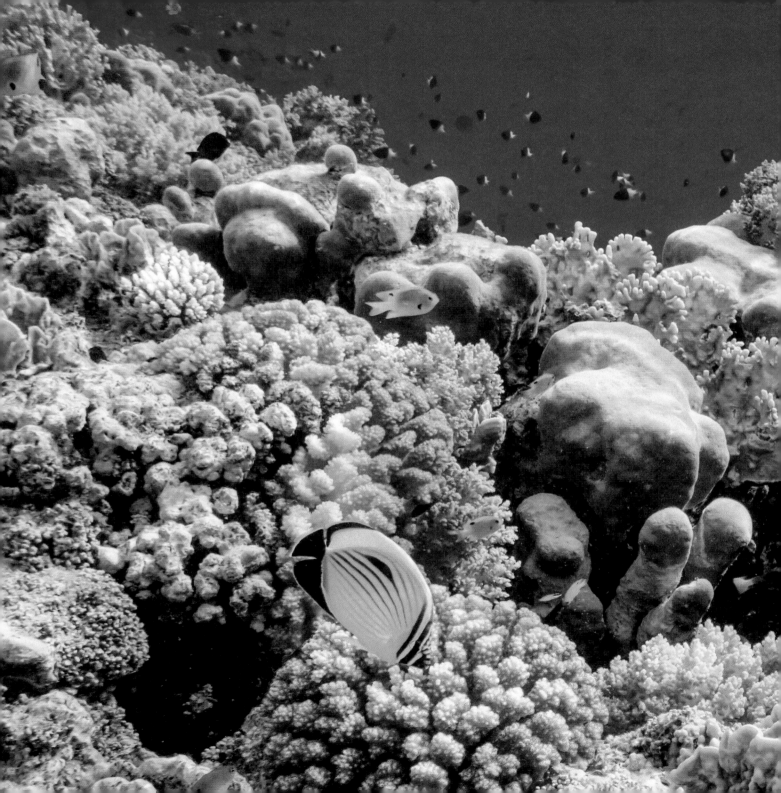

Colorful Coral Reef on Red Sea nearby Marsa Alam

THE CORAL REEF

When you first look at one, you might believe it is made from rocks. However, they are living organisms that consist of tiny animals known as polyps. The polyps reside outside of the reef. As they die, they then become hard and new polyps will grow on top of them. This is how they grow.

The different species of coral can be found in many different shapes and sizes. Some will look like flowers, honeycombs, fans, trees, mushrooms, and yes, even brains.

A calcareous skeleton forms when the polyps secrete calcium carbonate. Zooxanthellae is the host algae that works with the calcareous exo-skeleton. These single celled tiny algae are packed tightly within each cell contained in the coral tissue which is what gives the coral its color. They take in carbon dioxide and give off oxygen, through photosynthesis, which is then used by the host polyp.

Group of coral fish blue water.

If the temperature is hot for too long, this relationship collapses. If the high temperatures are only around for a short time, the remaining algae can divide rapidly providing relief for the coral and its color returns and the coral survives. Under extended times of stressful conditions, zooxanthellae will not reproduce, and many coral reefs proceed to die.

Coral formations in Queensland Ocean - Australian Coral Reef.

Coral Garden.

HOW DOES THE CORAL REEF SURVIVE?

In order to stay alive, these polyps have to eat. This is what feeds the reef. They feed on algae and tiny animals known as plankton. The sun provides the food for the algae by the process of photosynthesis. This explains why they tend to form closer to the water's surface and in water that is clear so that the sunlight can get through to provide food for the algae.

When the water gets too warm or too salty, these reefs will lose their algae and turn white.

WHERE ARE THEY LOCATED?

Coral reefs have to have shallow, warm water in order to form. These formations occur near coastlines closer to the equator and are also found close to islands throughout the world. A large portion of our coral reefs are found near Australia and Southeast Asia. The Great Barrier Reef, located near Australia, is considered to be the largest of the coral reefs, stretching for 2,600 miles. It is big enough to be seen from outer space.

Ocean sea fan.

Coral Reefs are typically located in tropical, clear oceans. They form in the waters from approximately 150 feet deep up to the surface of the water. They have to be able to receive light from the sun in order to live.

Underwater coral reef.

Reef-building corals flourish on a fringing reef in Fiji.

THREE TYPES OF CORAL REEFS

The three types of coral reefs are listed here:

FRINGE REEF – These are reefs that grow closer to the shore. They can be at the shore or there might be a lagoon or channel between the reef and the land, most often found in the Caribbean and Hawaii.

BARRIER REEF – These are reefs that grow further away from the shore, sometimes many miles away from the shore. Barrier reefs are found mostly in the Caribbean and the Indo-Pacific.

Great Barrier Reef from the sky.

ATOLL - An atoll consists of a ring of coral that is surrounding a body of water, like a lagoon. It begins as a fringe reef surrounding a volcanic island. While the coral grows, the island will then sink into the ocean, leaving only the coral. Sometimes, people can live on them since they can be so huge. These are typically found in the Indo-Pacific.

Coral Reef Atoll.

Coral reef in low tide in island, Indonesia.

CORAL REEF ZONES

Coral reefs will develop zones after a certain time period. Each of these zones is inhabited by different species of fish, corals, and other ocean life.

SHORE OR INNER REEF ZONE - This is the area between the shoreline and the crest. Dependent upon the size and shape of the reef, it can be full of fish, starfish, anemones, sea cucumbers, and other life

CREST REEF ZONE - This is known as the reef's highest point and where waves break over the reef.

FORE OR OUTER REEF ZONE - As the wall of reef begins to fall, the waters will get calmer. Generally, at approximately 30 feet deep, you will find the parts of the reef which are most populated as well as lots of different coral species.

Crown-of-thorns Starfish.

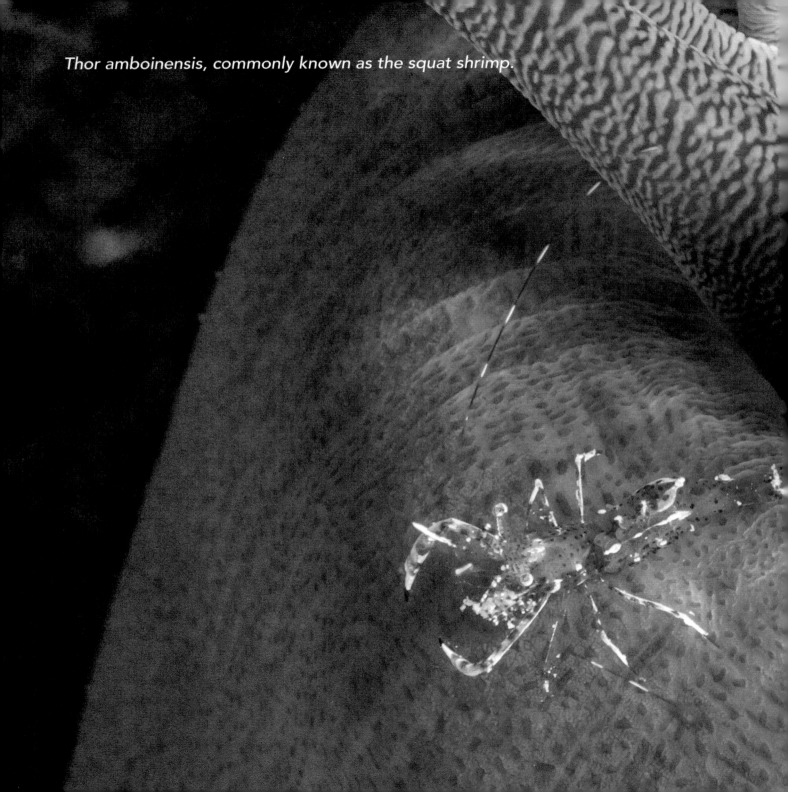

Thor amboinensis, commonly known as the squat shrimp.

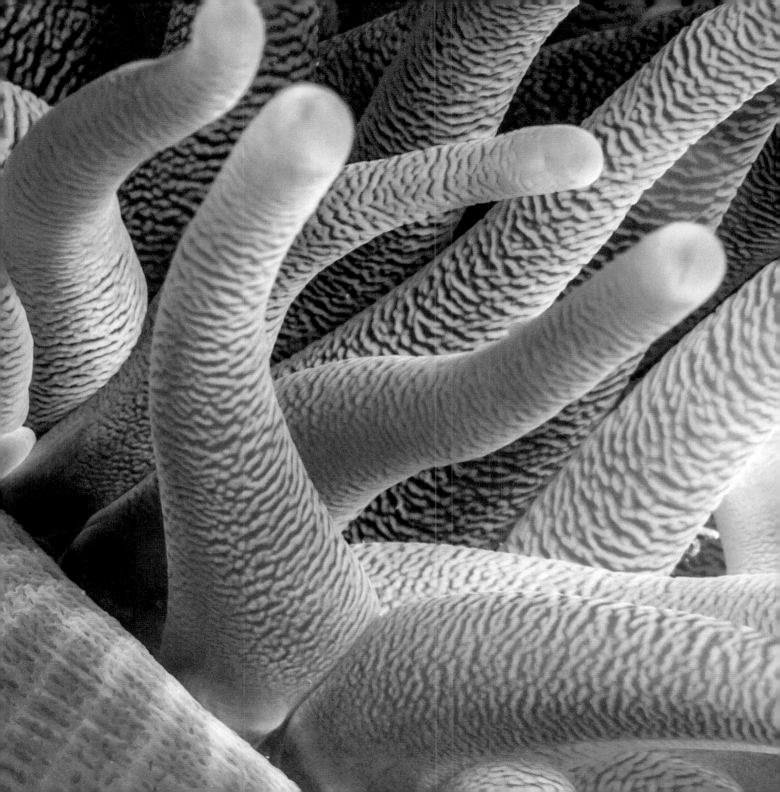

ANIMALS

Many kinds of animals live around these reefs. This includes different kinds of coral, including finger coral, cactus coral, column coral, brain coral, and star coral. Some of the animals rely upon each other to survive. This is known as a symbiotic relationship. Anemone and clown fish are an example of a symbiotic relationship.

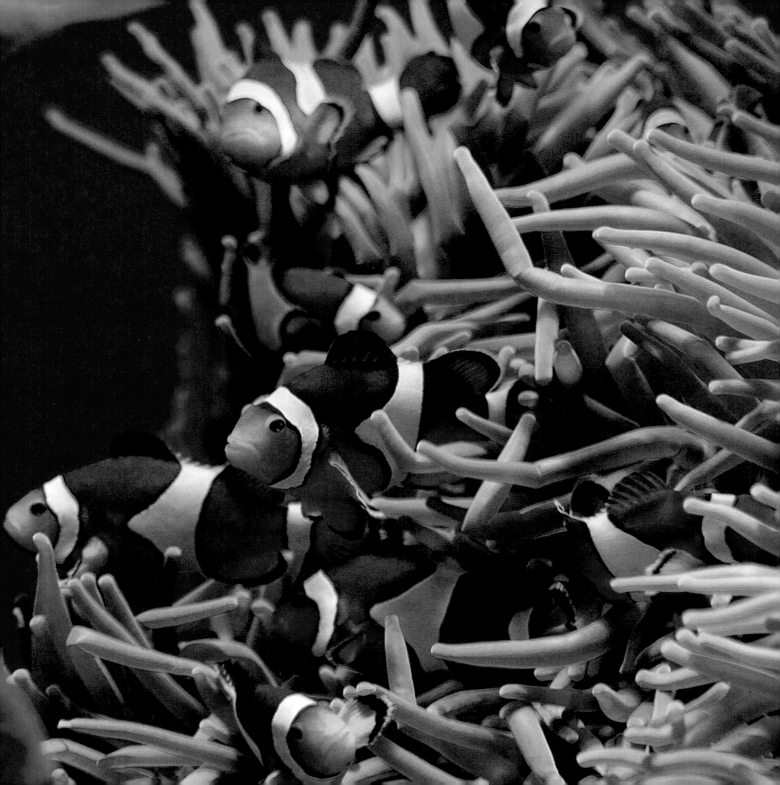

Additionally, some of the strangest and most interesting creatures of the world call it home. Several of these animals will attach to the reef and cover almost every square inch. These include clams, snails, cucumbers, anemones, starfish, and sponges. You will also find several different types of fish swimming around including eels, clownfish, pufferfish, lionfish, sharks, and cuttlefish. There are at least 1500 different species of fish and more than 400 species of coral that reside on Australia's Great Barrier Reef alone.

Clownfish Colony.

PLANTS

Most of the plants that call the coral reef home are different species of algae, seaweed, and sea grass.

Eelgrass Bed.

WHY ARE THEY IMPORTANT?

Besides being a vital part of our planet, as well as being a tourist attraction, being stunning, they also have a positive impact on people throughout the world, including food from fishing, protecting our coastlines from erosion, and even useful in medicines.

Coral reef underwater life.

ARE THEY IN PERIL?

Yes, they are being slowly destroyed. Due to the amount of time it takes for them to grow, they are currently disintegrating quicker than they are repaired. Much of this damages is by humans, primarily from overfishing and pollution. Tourists even damage them by touching them, standing on top of them, and bumping them with their vessels.

Environmental problem: old fishing net abandoned on coral reef

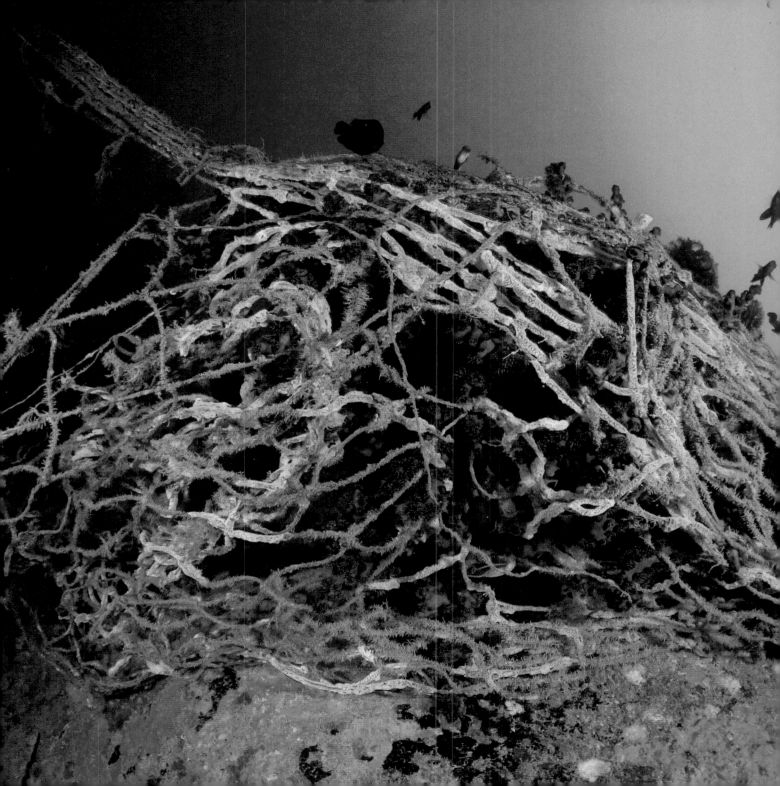

CORAL REEFS AND PEOPLE

Coral reef ecosystems are vital for numerous reasons. They remove and then recycle the carbon dioxide, which is a gas that contributes to global warming. In addition, they also protect our land from the harsh weather by absorbing the effect from strong storms and waves. They provide us with food, for example, conch and lobster. Coral reefs are a great tourist attraction. They provide great source of biodiversity

A diver explores the cracks, crevices and holes in a coral reef on the island of Grand Cayman.

Without reefs, many animals and plants will die. Reefs also yield some biological treasures which are becoming increasingly recognized as a natural source providing biomedical chemicals that have an encouraging future in the pharmacological industry. They can provide vital medicines, and even parts of their skeletons can be used as a substitute for bones in a reconstructive surgery.

Coral reefs provide a powerful educational tool. By learning about coral reefs, we can learn about ecosystems and biomes, and the interrelationship between these organisms and their environment.

For additional information on coral reefs, as well as other parts of the ecosystem, research the internet, go to your local library, and ask questions of your teachers, family, and friends.

Made in the USA
Middletown, DE
14 November 2021